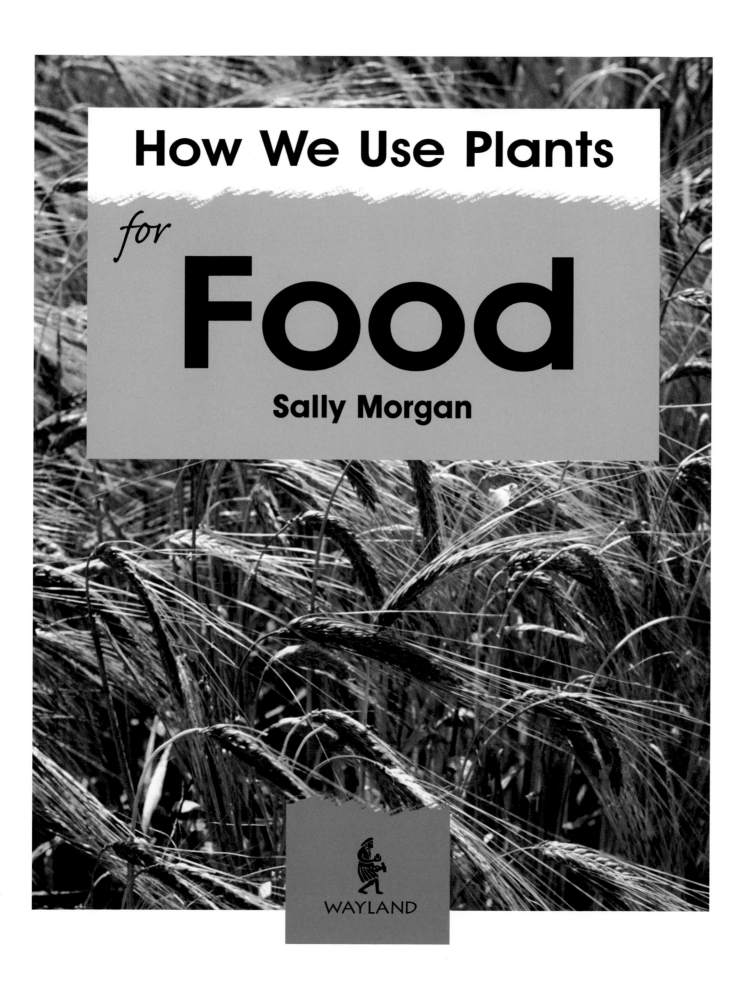

How We Use Plants

for

Food

Sally Morgan

WAYLAND

First published in 2007 by Wayland

Copyright © Wayland 2007

Wayland
338 Euston Road
London NW1 3BH

Wayland Australia
Level 17/207 Kent Street
Sydney, NSW 2000

Editor: Camilla Lloyd
Designer: Matthew Lilly
Picture Researcher: Sally Morgan

Picture Acknowledgments: The author and publisher
would like to thank the following for allowing these
pictures to be reproduced in this publication.
Cover: Inga Spence/Getty Images (main); Ecoscene.
Ecoscene: 1, 4, 5, 6, 7, 8, 9, 10, 11, 12, 13, 14,
15, 16, 17, 18, 19, 20, 21, 23, 24, 25, 26;
Steve Lupton/Corbis: 22; Mike Watson Images/Corbis: 26
(main); WR Publishing/Alamy: 26 (right); Bennett Dean; Eye
Ubiquitous/Corbis: 28.

With special thanks to Ecoscene.

British Library Cataloguing in Publication Data:
Morgan, Sally
How we use plants for food
1. Plants, Edible - Juvenile literature
I. Title
581.6'32

ISBN: 978 07502 5063 4

Printed in China

Wayland is a division of Hachette Children's Books

Contents

Plants for food

Plants are found almost everywhere – in gardens and parks, in the countryside and in the sea. They are not just attractive to look at, they are essential to our everyday lives as they provide us with much of our food.

This vegetable stall in a Malaysian market sells many types of plant foods including tomatoes, cabbage and chillis.

It's A Question!

How many different types of plants used as food can you find in your kitchen?

4

Plants are **organisms** that can make their own food in their **leaves**. The leaves trap sunlight and use it to make foods such as sugar and **starch**.

Around the world millions of hectares of farmland are used to grow crops such as wheat, maize and barley.

Animals cannot make their own food, so all animals, including people, rely on plants for food. **Herbivores** are animals that eat plant foods only. **Omnivores** are animals that eat a mixed **diet** of plant and animal foods. The meat-eating animals, such as lions, do not eat plants, but they hunt the herbivores and omnivores that do eat plants.

Cereals

Cereals are grasses with long, thin leaves. Examples of cereals include rice, wheat, barley and maize. The seed of a cereal is oval in shape. Around the outside is a tough seed coat that protects the seed inside.

Rice is planted in fields called paddies which are flooded with water.

The seed contains starch, a substance that is rich in energy. The starch is used by the seed when it **germinates** (starts to sprout) and grows into a new plant.

Did You Know?

White rice is rice that has had the seed coat removed, leaving just the white starch. Brown rice has the seed coat left on. Take a grain of brown rice and scrape off the brown seed coat. You should see white starch underneath.

Cereals are described as **staple** foods. They are full of energy and cheap to buy. They make up a large part of the diet of people around the world.

Cereal seeds contain starch and vitamins, especially vitamin B.

The combine harvester cuts the crop at ground level and shakes out the seeds.

Using cereals

Wheat and other cereals are used to make flour. The seeds are ground between rollers so that the seed coats are separated from the starch. Then the starch is ground into a fine powder that is called flour. Flour is used to make bread, pasta, biscuits and cakes.

All of the seed is used to make wholemeal flour.

When you mix water into flour it becomes sticky. This is because the flour contains a substance called **gluten**. Gluten is very elastic and is essential for making bread.

The left over bits of seed coat form **bran**. Bran is used in foods, such as breakfast cereals. **Wholemeal** flour has a brown colour because it contains bran and starch.

Have A Go!

Find out more about gluten by making a dough from flour and water.

● Place a few tablespoons of flour in the bowl and mix in a little water using your fingers.

● The **dough** sticks to your fingers. See how elastic it is by pulling the dough into different shapes.

Bread is a staple food. Many types of bread are on sale in this shop.

9

Vegetables

Vegetables come from all parts of the plant. For example, carrots are **roots**, tomatoes are **fruits**, cabbages and spinach are leaves and celery is a **stem**.

Have A Go!

Plants draw up water through tiny tubes in the stem. You can see this using coloured water.

- Put the cut end of a stem of celery in some water that has been coloured with food dye.

- After a couple of hours remove the celery and cut the stem in half across the middle. You should see tiny specks of colour. This is because the coloured water has been drawn up through the stem.

The type of vegetables on sale vary according to the time of year.

Plant foods contain tough fibres that are not broken down in the **gut**. Fibre helps food to move through the gut.

Vegetables are rich in **vitamins** and **minerals**. These are things that are needed in small quantities by the body. If the diet lacks a particular vitamin or mineral, the person may become ill or suffer from a disease. For example, spinach and broccoli are rich in iron, which is needed to make red blood cells.

Cabbages are full of vitamins and minerals.

Fruits

Fruits appear on a plant after the flowers have died. Seeds form inside the fruit. The fruit protects and nourishes the seeds. When a fruit is ripe, it splits open and the seeds are released.

There is a saying that an apple a day keeps the doctor away!

Many fruits are brightly coloured or taste sweet. This is to attract animals that carry the fruits away. The seeds are dropped over a large area. The pod of a bean or a pea plant is a fruit too as it is full of seeds.

12

Everybody should eat at least five portions of fruit and vegetables a day.

Fruits can be eaten raw or cooked or squeezed to make a juice. Fruits are healthy foods because they contain vitamins and minerals, for example oranges are rich in vitamin C.

Did You Know?
The world's sweetest fruit is the Carabao Mango.

13

Keeping food fresh

Many fruits become sweeter and softer as they ripen. However, once they are ripe, they soon go soft and mouldy.

As tomatoes get more ripe they become sweeter and more juicy.

Fruits and vegetables have to be transported quickly from farms to shops. Often they are stored in cool rooms to keep them fresh. Nowadays, many salad vegetables are sold ready-prepared in bags. The bags keep out the air so the salad leaves stay fresh for longer.

Bananas turn from green to yellow as they ripen.

Have A Go!

See how long lettuce leaves stay fresh under different conditions.

• Take 9 lettuce leaves and three small clear plastic bags. Place three lettuce leaves in each bag. Squash the bags to get rid of the air and seal the bag. Place one bag on a window ledge, another in a dark cupboard and the third one in the fridge.

• Check them every day. Do not open the bag but just look through the plastic. Which leaves stay fresh for longest?

Preserving plant food

Many fruits and vegetables are seasonal. This means that they are only available at a certain time each year, for example apples are **harvested** in autumn. There are ways of **preserving** plant foods so that they can be eaten at other times of the year. A simple way is to dry fruits and vegetables in the sun.

These apricots and apples are drying in the sun in Pakistan.

Another way of preserving fruits and vegetables is by making jams and chutneys. Jam is made by boiling fruit and sugar together until it turns thick and can be poured into jars. Chutney is a savoury pickle made from vegetables such as tomatoes.

Preserved fruits and vegetables are sold in this Brazilian shop.

It's A Question!

Which fruits are dried to make prunes?

Fruits and vegetables can be stored in a sealed bottle or metal can. This keeps air away from the food so that it does not go off. Frozen plant foods can be kept in a freezer for many months.

Seeds

A seed grows into a new plant. Seeds are useful foods because they are rich in starch, protein and fat. Cereal seeds are not the only important seeds. There are many other useful examples, such as sunflower and sesame seeds.

Sunflower seeds from the head of the flower can be eaten whole, raw or cooked, added to breads or sprinkled over salads.

All nuts have a hard shell. The edible part of the nut is found inside.

A nut is usually a hard-shelled seed. Nuts are nutritious plant foods. The coconut is an important plant food in **tropical** areas. The nut is found inside a hairy husk. The inside of the nut is filled with a white flesh. Coconut milk is made by squeezing the flesh into water. It is used often in spicy tropical dishes. Both the coconut flesh and milk are rich in protein, fats and carbohydrates.

Plant oils

Many fruits and seeds are rich in oil. The oil can be removed from the plant and used in many ways. Olive oil is used in cooking. Sunflower oil can be made into margarine.

Have A Go!

It is easy to see how much oil is in a seed.

- Take a sunflower seed and crush it between two sheets of white paper. Can you see an oil stain on the paper?

Olives can be pressed to make olive oil which is used in cooking and salad dressings.

Two common plant oils are soybean and oil palm. They are used in many food products, as well as detergents and soaps.

Oil from oil seed rape is used as a cooking oil.

Oils and fats are similar things. However, a fat is solid or semi-solid at room temperature while an oil is liquid. Butter and lard are animal fats while margarine is usually made from vegetable oils.

In South East Asia oil palm is used as cooking oil and as an ingredient in a wide range of foods.

Herbs and spices

Herbs and **spices** are added to food to give flavour, taste or colour. They come from different parts of plants. Vanilla comes from the seed pod of the vanilla orchid, while cinnamon comes from the bark of the cinnamon tree.

Indian foods, such as this Chicken Tikka Masalla, are often spicy. They contain spices like cumin, coriander and garlic.

It's A Question!

Paprika is a type of spice. From which plant is it made?

Herbs tend to be green and come from the leafy parts of plants. Parsley, mint, rosemary and thyme are used to flavour foods. Usually a spice is full of flavour. Spices come from the hard parts of the plant. Cloves are dried flower buds, black peppers are berries, while ginger comes from a root.

Only about 10 or so threads of saffron are needed to give colour to a bowl of rice.

The most expensive spice in the world is saffron. Saffron gives food a bright yellow-orange colour and an intense licorice flavour. Saffron is used in **paella**. Saffron is made from part of the crocus flower.

Sugar from plants

Sugar is a sweet-tasting substance that is made by all plants. However, two types of plants produce large quantities of sugar. They are sugar cane and sugar beet.

This sugar cane crop is being harvested by a machine. In some parts of the world, it is harvested by hand.

Sugar beet is related to the beetroot. This sugar beet plant produces a swollen root that is rich in sugar.

Sugar cane is grown in tropical areas. Each year, the stems of sugar cane are harvested and taken to a sugar mill. The stems are crushed to make the juice.

The juice is heated so the water **evaporates**. This leaves behind brown crystals of sugar. This brown sugar can be refined (treated further) to leave pure white granulated sugar.

Did You Know?
In South Asia, pieces of sugar cane are sold as sweets from street stalls. The pieces are chewed to release a sugary syrup.

How the tomato plant is used

The fruits of the tomato plant can be used in many different ways. Tomatoes produce a cluster of fruits called a truss. The fruits are green at first. Then they turn yellow. Finally the fruits turn red, which is a sign that the fruit is ripe. However, not all tomatoes are red. Some types of tomato produce white, yellow or stripy orange fruits.

Puree and paste:
Tomatoes can be cooked and strained to form a tomato puree. A tomato paste is made by cooking tomatoes for several hours, so that they form a thick, concentrated paste. The paste can be used in many sauces and meat dishes.

Canned:
Fresh tomatoes can be preserved by canning. A can of tomatoes will keep for several years.

Fresh:
Tomatoes can be eaten raw, in salads or as a snack.

Juice:
The fruits can be pressed to make a juice.

27

Make your own sun-dried tomatoes!

A single tomato plant can produce many tomatoes that can be eaten, made into a puree, juiced or dried in the sun.

Step 1

Buy a small tomato plant in early summer. Plant it in a pot and place it outside in a sunny place. Tomatoes grow tall so put a stake in the pot. As the tomato plant grows taller secure the stem to the stake. Remove any side shoots.

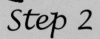

Step 2

Make sure you water your tomato regularly. Tomatoes grow fast and need plenty of nutrients, so you may need to feed it with a plant food. There are special tomato feeds that you can buy in garden centres.

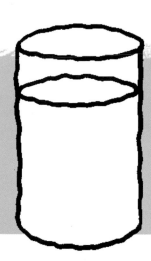

Tomato juice

Once you have some ripe tomatoes you can make some tomato juice by putting some tomatoes into a juicer. You can make the tomato juice a bit more spicy by adding a few drops of Worcester sauce.

Step 3

You can make sun-dried tomatoes. Pick some small tomatoes and cut them in half. Blot them dry with a paper towel and place them on a wire rack. You can leave the wire rack on a warm, sunny window ledge for a couple of days.

Step 4

When the tomatoes are dry, they should be leathery and a bit like a raisin in texture. Store them in a jar with an air-tight lid or in a sealed plastic bag. They keep for up to six months. When you want to use the tomatoes, soak them in hot water for about 10 minutes. Ask an adult to help you.

Glossary

bran the separated seed coats of cereals.

diet the mix of foods eaten by a person or animal.

dough a mix of flour and water.

evaporate to change from a liquid into steam.

fruit the seed-bearing part of a plant.

germinate to sprout from a seed.

gluten an elastic substance found in flour.

gut part of a person's digestive system.

harvested ripened crops that have been gathered from the fields.

herb the leafy part of a plant used to flavour food.

herbivore an animal that eats plants.

leaf (pl leaves) part of a plant, a blade that is attached to the stem.

mineral a natural substance found in vegetables. The body needs small amounts of minerals.

omnivore an animal that eats both animals and plant foods.

organism a living thing, such as a plant, animal or bacteria.

preserving treating a food in such a way so it can be kept for longer.

paella a Spanish dish made with rice, seafood, chicken and vegetables and flavoured with saffron.

roots the underground parts of a plant.

spice strongly flavoured part of a plant used to give food colour or taste.

staple an energy-rich food which forms a large part of the diet, for example, rice and potato.

starch a carbohydrate found in plant foods such as cereals and potatoes. Starch gives us energy.

stem part of a plant that supports the leaves.

tropical areas of the world which lie close to the Equator and which are hot all year round.

vitamin a nutrient needed by the body in small amounts.

wholemeal a flour that is made from the whole grain.

Further information

Books

Looking at Plants, Flowers, Fruits and Seeds by Sally Morgan, Belitha Press, 2002

How does your Garden Grow? Great Gardening for green-fingered kids by Clare Matthews and Clive Nichols, Hamlyn Gardening, 2005

Websites

The Fruit Pages:
http://www.thefruitpages.com/
Website with lots of information about fruit.

Oxfam Cool Planet:
http://www.oxfam.org.uk/coolplanet/kidsweb /world/ethiopia/ethoxf1.htm
Website for the charity Oxfam with pages of food projects from around the world.

The Great Plant Escape:
http://www.urbanext.uiuc.edu/gpe/
Web pages packed with information about plants and why they are important to our lives. Quizzes to test your knowledge.

Answers

P15 the lettuce leaves in the fridge

P17 plums

P22 sweet red pepper

Index